Bonsai Love

Bonsai Love

poems

Diane Tucker

HARBOUR PUBLISHING

Harbour Publishing Co. Ltd.
P.O. Box 219, Madeira Park, BC, V0N 2H0
www.harbourpublishing.com

Edited by Elaine Park
Cover photograph by Venucci Pty. Ltd.
Cover design by Carleton Wilson
Text design by Mary White
Printed and bound in Canada

Harbour Publishing acknowledges financial support from the Government of Canada through the Canada Book Fund and the Canada Council for the Arts, and from the Province of British Columbia through the BC Arts Council and the Book Publishing Tax Credit.

Cataloguing data available from Library and Archives Canada
ISBN 978-1-55017-643-8 (paper)
ISBN 978-1-55017-644-5 (ebook)

To all the ones the tiny girl has ever loved.

"I fear to love you, Sweet, because
Love's the ambassador of loss."

— *Francis Thompson*

Contents

Prologue: Eve as rib

If time could be wound back before clock,
before sundial, almost before sun,
I'd spend a day, if I could, as your rib,
suspended awhile before God drew me out.

You stand after a strenuous morning of naming,
the unnamed still rubbing themselves
against your calves in the wordless new air.

You stretch and spread your fingers
across me while gazing into the distance
at that blueness we'll call "mountains."

A big sheepish sort of creature rubs
against you then, and so against me,
both of us poked, both nudged for a name
or for its absence, not even this beast
wanting words right now, no word to slip
like a waxy leaf between it and its beginning.

Your hand still spread-eagled along my length,
they dawn on you, dawn in you: hunger and thirst.

So I help hold you in and up all the way
to the water and the fruit; I hang there,
stretched piece of your heart's bone-basket,
spine-sconced white hook, marrow-cored
blood coffer cuddling a lung in the dark.
When, that night, you lay down to sleep,

there's an insomniac hour. A sensation
we'll later, together, name *pain* licks your side.

Brand new, it keeps you awake but somehow
isn't unpleasant yet. You press your hand against
the place that seems to pulse the strange feeling.
Pain, unfallen, is your body making ready.
You become sure of this. You careen toward sleep
curled around the place, both hands clutching it.

Something is going to happen, you think,
when the sun burns and I make words again
for the creatures. Perhaps (your last waking thought)
I'll hear the sound of my own name spoken
at last by one of these wandering beasts?

Biology Class

The circulatory system of the rat was too small,
arteries thready and ruinable by study, so they
shipped us bullfrogs. These ones three times
the size of the rats, their Louisiana hearts big enough,
their veins and valve connections more visible.

On each frog's belly, cuts had been made
that opened its torso like a book, front cover
and back, and its story was all there on one deep page.
We read it from beginning to end, the blood chapter,
anyway (though all their blood had been poured out
to keep the lab clean, dissectors' hands unstained).

In the lab's remaining minutes we could read
whatever else of the frog we wanted; so we read
the food chapter, our scalpels tracing slits
across each beastie's tightly packed stomach,
and there (book within a book!) curled a crayfish
bigger than a big man's thumb, its many legs
and eyes on stalks perfectly preserved as well,
swallowed but not a jot digested.

Poor bullfrog (or not, his last moments spent
snagging and slurping down this fine crustacean
filet), guts up on the lab bench, his elegantly curved
chin a dead, shiny grey in the flat classroom light.

What would we, the dissectors, divulge
from our dark body cavities if you got us pinned

to that waxen slab? What would you find
stuffed in our nineteen-year-old guts?

The last things we took in before they got us,
I imagine: swollen, overworked hearts, fresh
as the night we snapped them shut inside us;
arms and legs that held us close; spines of jelly;
larynxes choked with the unsaid and the unrepeatable.

What crazy school let *us* (eyes staring, tongues
dry and graceless, lips bruised with backroom kissing,
brains red and puddled in our anxious pants)
peek into the books of the soft and harmless
with handfuls of small sharp objects?

The Deck

You wore a pig-suede
bomber jacket, soft, in forest green.
Each of your Dutch-boy eyes shone like chestnut
silk, two gold-brown discs gathering the dying light.

Those two were set in skin pristine as a newborn's,
pale and seemingly untouched, except your cheeks,
always high-coloured as if freshly slapped.

Everything made of bone in you
was pleasingly rounded: nose and chin, sweet pale
forehead, high skull with its deep bark-brown hair
swept across in a heavy, gleaming bang.

That's what I remember, and some pleasing
imperfection in your teeth that made your
round-lipped smile a slightly diagonal surprise.

The way we sat on a high stone wall and talked
until we realized we were stiff with cold. You jumped
down, held me as I jumped and then kept holding.

Autumn was our first season. Always outside, you
in your jacket, thick and green as laurel leaves, me
in my old black coat, soft and wide as a fat man's
evening shadow. We leaned into each other's outerwear.

But here's where the fine crack runs up memory's wall:
that black coat, the best coat I've ever had, I didn't own

that coat for at least another year. Or did I? How I hate
this shuffling of the deck: I can be sure of so much less
when I remember. Months and years are amputated
and sewn bloodily onto the wrong stumps: all this past
must be a sort of butchered freak, all its parts in attendance
but disordered, like Brueghel's passel of limb-warped
beggars, low to the ground and limping. So, I apologize.

I remember myself only as I wish I'd been.
That black coat made me an agile city cat. It made me
knowing and complete. I think it was made of
cartoon portable hole: whenever I put it on,
whoever touched it would disappear inside me,
be held in me forever.

That must be what I wanted from you:
to have you closer than mere Student Union
would allow. To be filled with your whole forest-green
self, your autumn-chill eyes, your dark hair folded
across your high forehead in a heavy, quivering wing.

Cup

When our hands are small and cannot lift one up,
our mothers and fathers help us drink the milk-filled cup.

A father kneels, stares silently at his crying son,
takes the small face between his hands, a pearl in a cup.

There is no question – the first love is a crown of thorns,
kisses like the dusty-throated seeking the rim of the cup.

A concave world sinks and narrows to a ring
scummed in fine brown dregs, the fragrant coffee cup.

Eye to eye, speaking softly over the rising steam, hearts
are given and taken with a word, palms around warm cups.

Nothing fills every cranny like this shared meal:
bread torn and passed along; wine from the common cup.

True love is a transplant. It slices us open
and replaces vital organs. Dare we drain this cup?

Long before starvation, thirst will have killed you.
Wine in silver or water in two palms, take and empty the cup.

Tonight

Tonight I'm a machine,
run down; a camera shooting,
shooting, with no eye behind it.

All the parts work
but there is no sum of them
to be greater than.
A Rube Goldberg, a useless
cartoon contraption.

Don't ask
what the machine produces:
noise, movement, the occasional
pleasant spark.

The night sky
is a layer of wet earth on me.
Rain: solid grains of chilled air.
The street is a long tunnel.
The urge to burrow up is futile tonight.
Even the mountaintops are buried.

No use saying I want *someone*
to be with; not unless it's the *right*
someone, a fellow sad worm
interested in nothing but clinging
to this darkness, to this darkness
hanging on to us like roots.

"The Windhover" by Heart

I heard you speak it
and fell in love
in a breath, stone
falling into water
irresistible as gravity

there it's remained
ever since, stone
at the bottom
of a deep deep well

no weed clings there
no filth finds purchase
no current erodes
o smooth white stone

it emits a gentle
a steady small light
the deep's chill
can't pierce its warmth

as beautiful
as the day
it descended
it keeps me
from hitting
the very bottom

o warmth
o light
o smooth
white stone

Dearest…

...of morning and evening solitude,
of long walks under the small-leafed trees
full of afternoon owls.

Dearest of the liquid pewter-grey inlet,
of the steep hill, the small house,
the sunlit stream, its small fires
passing like processions of quick candles.

Dearest voice, dearest lines of words
laid out for bewildered me to follow,
breadcrumbs in a black and bird-infested wood.

Dearest of contemplation,
of staring into space, of keeping mum on the bus
all the way there and all the way back, of tucking
truth in the brain's secret folds
like money between old books' leaves.

Dearest of silence,
of no words, of before and after the visit,
of walking home alone, of the closed door,
the curtained window, the empty bed.

Dearest of nowhere and nobody: never,
not at all, nothing, nada, dearest dark *niente*.

Contrail

gashed across the blue
a knife wound seeping white

No telling when I'll see you
again, if ever. I cannot know,
so I save you up behind my eyes.
Then I can conjure you in a second
and have you sitting next to me.

from back end to front
it bleeds itself blue again, thinning,
widening, until it lets clouds
and fistfuls of flung geese
through its veil

You won't like it
but I dream of your father.
I've never met him, know him
only by nasty reputation,
but he's your father.

it arches, its end planted
in the horizon of the hill
it collects the late orange light
and the surrounding blue, aspiring
to be a rainbow

Whatever of your father
that's made its way into you,

that I love. Your hands,
that you once said were the same
as his hands; I love those hands.

instead it's a white bow, a smoke bow,
a path marked but fading

His sadness. The crying animal
inside the barbed-wire ball of himself.

triangular cirrostratus
one wide lacy wing
riding the updraft blue

Are you caught halfway out,
a foot still lodged, twisted,
or did you just ball up
all that wire even smaller
and swallow him down?

cirrostratus pulled cotton-candy thin:
a threadbare veil, one white lick of paint,
the sky drybrushed and thirsting

"In the Nocturnal Garden"

after the print by Graham Walker

Subterranean in the sun,
at moonrise this garden shows its face,
casts off columns of earth and rises in white rows.

Books grow, their thousand leaves fanning open
in the night light, showing their shining faces,
each letting loose a bright ascending star.

Book leaves open and turn for the stalks of eyes
that, rising, see what happens in the dark.
They know. In the black and silver soil of silence,
lie still. You are seen. You are known.

The Book of Everything

The book of everything
would be blank, don't you see?
Molecules mashed together without end
would make a white plane of stardust,
all matter's old mother.

The book of everything
would be elliptical, a bound galaxy
you could roll across the surface of the sea.
When opened, it would cover
the Sahara with dripping flowers.

Go through your days with a big eraser
and divest that book of everything bitter.
Write sugar there. Write spices.
Write heavy bread and butter and salt.

Open your eyes every morning
and let me look into them. There
I will read a book of everything
I was ever given to love.

Ovation Balladeer

The classical guitarist in the long black coat
is playing the same kind of guitar you have,
the one you've played for twenty years.

There's his guitar case on the pavement,
the case I know so well. I toss in a dollar,
but it bounces out. I have to pick it up
and toss it in again. Maybe I did that
on purpose, to be close to that case,

to the case's marigold lining; I always loved
that guitar case with that velvet lining.
I wanted to lay down in it. I know

how you have to carry a guitar lovingly,
as you'd hold a baby or a sleeping woman,
and how you have to handle the guitar's
shoulders and long perfect neck
(the things we make out of wood
sometimes more sinuous than sinew).

Who wouldn't want a neck as beautiful
as a guitar's? A neck never touched without
care, attention, a longing to understand,
fret by fret, string by taut, fingered string.

Who wouldn't want her whole self rehearsed
from top to bottom, in every key, before being
laid down to rest in a marigold velvet bed?

Tuning up

Your hands have all the right calluses,
rough and smooth in the proper harmony.

Right now the rough is picking out notes
on the keyboard; the smooth is plucking,
turning the head's keys, tuning.

Sunlight is splashed down the living room walls
like a June morning striking San Marco sideways.

When everything is in tune and you're ready
to play, can I sing along? Can we pick up
and go? Can we find that very thickness of light
on marble and make all our music there?

A short silence, a stillness (your hands, listening)
and you look up. It's as if, from behind your
small smile, the music is already ringing out.

Questions I Wish to Be Asked

1. Would you like to be done now,
finished speaking, finished calculating?

2. Would you like to start walking
and not stop until your knees buckle?

3. Would you like me to come over
and read to you, maybe a few dozen
Psalms, loudly, from a rooftop?

4. Then can we sing them?
Would you sing jazz songs with me
until we croak like a dry door?

5. Are there any musicals
we haven't sung the scores of yet?
Any hymns we have yet to learn?
Can we do it now?

6. Would you read me your poems
while I play you my mandolin,
my banjo, my ukulele, my banjolele,
my golden-hammered dulcimer?

7. Can you come up on this here cloud?

8. Can I play you my harp?

cover my mouth

on the hill by the lake
under the moon my mouth opens
a black O you cover with your own
and fill with silver

you are the lake's lithe black arms
clutching the moon's white light
clasping it firmly as the mountains hold
the lake, her spreading crow-black hair
between their thighs

come and cover my mouth again
stop my words on the dark green hill
while the lake moistens the mountains' lap
fill my throat with silver

Temple

In the temple of my heart I hold you

– Hakim Sanai

this ruin at my centre
this roofless cathedral
row of gap-toothed leaning buttresses
supporting emptiness

the church mice here nibble air
organ pipes hang dry and breathless

you can't tell the difference
between church and cemetery
all just rows of broken stones

but there is no end of room
stretch out on a pew and behold the sky
I grow moss here on the north side
of everything and drink the rain

there is plenty for you: pull
the clouds over
and wring them out for us

bread, cheese and apples

apples are flesh
are firm and yet yield
darken in the sun
have skin and thready pink veins
quartered they're pale, smooth
as the slope of your bare foot

cheese is flesh
the ripe flesh of your upper arm
the salt tang, the same
muscular resistance against the lips

bread is flesh
lets all in and digests it
carries, dear soaking trencher,
meats and all the juices
to their end –
its back broken and sliced
it is still flesh
the body made more whole
with every bite

Shadow

My shadow needs to put some
clothes on, but she doesn't give a damn.
Throw her a tablecloth if it's pretty
and she'll be happy enough.

Like all shadows, she ought to
stick to walls, stay underfoot,
but she insists on the centre of the
room: somewhere she can twirl.

Her feet know how to find
cool dry grass. Her arms are
strong and wiry and want
to pick things up and throw them.

I make her laugh, apparently:
my bluster and prevarication;
my shifting eyes. Today I won't take
her hand, but I keep watching.

It all makes her laugh and run
in circles, and chase the ice cream
truck down the street and catch it,
and buy its entire contents with kisses,
and feed all of it to the neighbourhood
cats and dogs, except for the rainbow
popsicles, which she eats herself, all except

the one she saves for me.

Hands

The starfish on our arms that live and move on land;
flippers sliced to form fingers: human hands.

Hands fly in front of us like shields at threat
or hurt; heraldic signs, splayed: warning hands.

"My hands are tied," we say when all avenues are shut,
the head and heart no use without the hands.

After birth they're counting the fish-roe fingers
that curl around everything close – a baby's hands.

No glove can warm, no hearthfire heat the soul,
like the silent, unsought grasp of a child's hand.

The wedding rings turned and turned on her
shrunken white bones, my grandmother's nighttime hands.

When the heart is desolate and despairs of receiving
the loved one, she can live on the sight of his hands.

Palm to palm is like a nakedness, heel to head.
Is the whole body recapitulated in the hands?

When we think of Christ, it's not the scourge or crown
that make us cringe – it's nails through the hands.

Divestiture: that's what the upturned palm is for.
It says: "Take what's there. Leave me two empty hands."

Why Don't You Take the Bus?

You don't want to touch
anyone, press too close.
The seats, you assert, are too small.

Does your small-boned body
feel the shudder of strange sorrows,
strangers' ambivalent breath
snaking into your own lungs?

May I urge you to sample
this particular propinquity?

Sit quietly beside the old
Ethiopian lady. Feel her heavy
round side against your own.
Don't break gaze with toddler
in the stroller, his quizzing eyes.
Fill your lungs with all the fetid
communal air; new flesh freshens it.

It is benefit and blessing,
bearing with broken others,
the weight and heft of every
other rider toward the sinking west.

When you arrive home
I will gather your small bones
against me. I will shake you free

of every lurching hesitation,
free of every rush and rattle.

And in the cloud of having touched,
we will lie flat and motionless
against each other's silent bodies,
hallowed and transported.

The Balcony

You like the stars best:
once known, they stay the same.
Known in the way you love to know:
names, positions,
how far from one another.

You walk back and forth
on the balcony, naming
as though introducing me
to some beloved relations:
"…my great aunt Cassiopeia,
cousins Castor and Pollux,
and Uncle Jupiter,
you must meet good old Jupiter."

I just wish you
and this crazy, cold family
would go away.
Equally possible, of course –
you going away
and Sirius going out, like a ski-run light
on a distant mountainside, snapped off.
I may as well wish away
my own legs.

This is why you like the stars:
they like you back.
This they prove by never moving,
staying where you can pin them

with your binoculars, match them to the chart,
be sure where they'll be tomorrow,
red and yellow and white, shimmering.

Finally alone on the balcony,
I push out breath in noisy puffs
to see the dull pewter
star-and-street light
reflect off my exhalations.
I prefer, I tell myself, to learn
without maps.

But the starfield tonight is all aloof,
full of closed faces, impenetrable.
The original cosmic clique.

Until one seems to sprout a tail,
etches a path over Saturn,
a fading, delicate arc,
then goes out.
I grip the balcony railing,
the thread of silver
a knifepoint across my heart.

It says *they move.*
It says *they fall.*
It says
if you watch
if you are faithful
the night may open.

The One I Love Is in Another Country

Why will the whole of love come on me suddenly
when I am sad and feel you are far away?
— Pablo Neruda, "Clenched Soul"

Christmas lights aren't helping anymore, not in the bowels of February.

Neither the yellow walls we painted together, nor their green spouses across the room.

I'll make a hot water bottle before bed, to keep my feet warm while the rain knocks all its foreheads against the skylight.

Sometimes, this night is saying from its dusty corners, *nothing helps.* Sometimes the maw stays gaping, light and colour impotent to fill it.

But that's okay. "No help" is a rest by the road, if you'll stop looking for another.

In this cold roadside of a night, it's shadow that feeds. The pussy willows' shadows catch and hold the pussy willows, making a black lattice of embraces up the yellow wall.

The ball of dog on the green couch, her black patches like shadows encroaching. She stays put as her dark spaces overtake her. She curls closer and breathes.

Why indeed move out from under it, out from under the Night of No One Else?

This night leaves a double emptiness, double room for the assertion of the inanimate, for bookcase and lamp to partner you.

The pen delivers, dragging out its inky umbilical line. It is the arrow pointing to every passable border.

It is, melting as it goes, the dark path of your footprints.

Glass Heart

Light comes through this heart as through ice,
ice thick enough to fish through, ice laced
with bubbles, frozen blue ripples, the path
of a tossed stone seized and etched, stalks
of grass twisted, turned blue and wired stiff
into the thick crystal.

Light comes through – light makes it, but just.
A wavy lilac-coloured light, its pearled surface
showing its age: crazed, reptile-skinned.

This heart is heavy to lift but small enough
to pocket and hide. Set down, its weight keeps
everything under it in place. It traps papers.
It holds a book open at the newly turned page.

Near the heart of this heart there is a knot
of ripples that turns back on itself, a pressed
whorl, a vortex of blue looking like nothing
if not a thumbprint. Turned the right way,
upward, toward the light, it throws back gold.

A dream

That the one inside you
and the one inside me
could find the path
that penetrates these woods.

That those two could separate
from us and be themselves,
clasping hands as they disappeared
into damp shadows.

The one inside me
who wants the one inside you
is patient most of the time,

but suffers a hollow
that wants moss and skin
and a clean, quick stream.

They are bodiless, these two
inside us who lean,
who crane toward one another

and ride rattling around
in us, revenging themselves
against our living bodies.

If they could get out of us,
if they could disappear
behind the high wall of shadows

we'd be free somehow,
you and I,
free to walk apart,

free to make our way
through the bright, baking city
and on into the penetrable day.

Jungian

Animus, you are the heavens.
A body of light; column of fire.
I am the earth, they tell me.
A body of darkness; a valley at night.

I am willing to be darkness to your light
if your fire will cleanse me. Willing
to be scraped empty. Scoured bare.
A stone, then. A tableland:
body of bare earth baked dry.

But this must be only the first meeting
of earth and sky. Between us, as our surfaces
press together, creation's children appear.
Born in the dark, but spreading toward light,
held up by the earth but nourished by water
and light from the sky.

The grass of the field is our union. The trees.
Green tendrils knit our two skins together.
Flowers smear the dirt and the air, our brief tattoos.

Sky begins in unimaginable height and falls
until it pools on the earth.
Earth begins in unimaginable depth and bubbles up
until it spreads against the sky.

And at this spherical horizon our wet, shaggy children
uncurl, take on mass, toss their hair and murmur

as their mother turns; bend and stretch as their father
passes his blinding hand over their faces.

In this picture, every man is an atmosphere
and every woman a depthless planet.
Together they make a world fit for life.
Sky with no earth is mere vapour.
Earth with no sky is a sterile stone.

The happy friction of the two sparks life,
this slippery, shining layer; this congress of green eons.

Too Much Feeling

Like eating all the flavours
of ice cream at once: desire,
melancholy, joy, fear, worry.
It all turns into one heavy grey
sludge in the bottom of the bowl.

That's the moment you
abandon your spoon, push away
from the table, head out the door.
You keep walking, keep walking,
until your gut is an empty bowl.

I Know What I Know

Will he carve us into his palms tonight? We need
a path deep enough for tears, that ancient river,
one strong enough to cut cities in us. Canyons.

The shadows are longer than I remember,
the chill sooner. Is the sun running faster?
What is he trying to get away from? His own corona?

Why should we ask all our questions at once?
Those answers will wait. They wait somewhere
under my tongue, dissolving. Search for them.

Why bother closing or hiding anything?
You know about the sun, how its heat bathes
the evil and the good. Inescapable baking.

The moon, where no water flows, is covered with seas
of Rains, Clouds, Moisture, each a plain of white dust.
The empty seas of Tranquility, Serenity, Knowledge. And Crises.

Tonight we feel everything that cuts us off
from the sky, from the chill bright parade of stars.
Tonight we are only what we cannot reach. Hands empty.

Even the birds are stuck down here, pecking
for what they can find in the streets, pretending
that stones from our shoes are seeds. That we might grow.

I know, damn it, I know what I know, and it's
not doing us any good anymore. Stop telling me.
When will we be more than we know? Like the birds.

The poor dry moon got up there somehow.
Somewhere there must be words that will serve
as stairs, as swords to cut the city free. As wings.

Coming Down with Something

Something is trying to make me sick,
lighting match after match in the back
of my throat, inhabiting my joints
with long, slow fire.

I ought to sleep, but cannot.

Do I speak things too intimate for you?
Are there lines I don't know I've crossed?
It's been years since I remembered my lines.

Are the shaking and the headaches
just the virus pounding to get in, or
are they echoes, damnable afterimages
of the things I wish I'd never said,
words I knew too smooth
as soon as they took flight to you,
or too rough, too raw, too much
like bare hands?

Leave the doctors their jargon.
I know this pain is the host
of my own detestable words
shoved back between my lips,
down my throat, and set to burning.

Beach glass

All of us were born
many times from this surf
and sucked back in,
our green and lilac
white and ochre shine
being scoured away,
all our sharp edges
rubbed strokably smooth.

We receive the sun
gratefully now, no longer
bouncing it all back at you.
We let it glaze our skin
softly, all of us etched
with a thousand tiny
light-collecting lines.

We've kept our curves
though, each of us shaped
like a human hand open
and at rest; each of us
carrying a little pool of
brine, an icy mouthful,
a doll-sized cup of what
the waves keep crying.

Pearl

Would I sell all I have, would I give the world
to purchase the Treasure, if I saw that Pearl?

The water holds me on my back, floating weightless
on the sea, gazed on from below by the bed of pearls.

They are perfect; I want them to be edible; I want to
burst them between my teeth, to swallow a nectar of pearls.

It is my mother's birthstone; in her dresser drawer
there are hinged boxes, gold and silver claws clasping pearls.

Poor Hamlet lost his mother to her unslaked thirst.
She insisted on drinking the cup that held the pearl.

I try to believe what you said about dogs and the sacred,
about being killed by pigs if I throw them my pearls.

They grow in darkness, airless, the fruit of irritation,
iridescent pain. When will my broken heart produce a pearl?

Touchless

In the dark the streetlight glows
on the narrow skeins of steam

ascending from the drying bay
of the bright, amazing, modern car wash:

touchless. If you happen to be a car,
no one lays a finger on you here

but the machines, the rag curtains,
the spinning brushes and ruthless jets,

the hot water and chemical foam
of your wordless cleansing, all full

of busy noise, with flashing lights,
red and green, directing you forward

through the preplanned starts and stops
of your whole hissing journey

from soil to shine. The perfect touchless shine.
Neither blot, nor streak, nor fingerprint:

flawless, not a single visible sign
that anything alive has ever touched you.

Nothing but steam in the bus loop lights;
nothing but the cloud of your perfection, drying.

The Fourth Direction

gloss on lines by Robert Bly

I do not know what will happen.
I have no claim on you.
I am one star
you have as guide; others
love you…

– from "The Indigo Bunting"

We are standing at the highest point of this green hill.
We see all there is to see in three directions. Behind us,
in the fourth, I do not know what will happen.

Everything is bright with a milky spring brightness,
all bathed in white light, but not blinding.
Suddenly your absence, your invisibility, is no threat.
The light opens my hands: I have no claim on you.

When we meet it is as the meeting of two stars
from the same constellation, neither of us at rest
unless we are light years apart. We anchor each other.
We make part of a picture. You assure me of my place
in the sky. I am one star you have as guide.

From this hilltop the city spreads at light speed
in three directions: the honeycomb houses; the black
inlet planted with boats, their masts a marsh of thin reeds;
the white skyscrapers, a forest of giant birches.
I can disappear from this green place in any direction
except the fourth: the mountains over my shoulder
looming like gods' blue fists, a mist where others love you.

The Balcony II

Just the Big Dipper.
It's the only one I can find myself
this close to summer.
I can follow the dipper's front
up to the North Star.
Not the biggest one, but always
there, they say.
Always hanging over the way north.

The rest of them my eyes try to gather
into pictures – a wing? An outstretched
neck? A water jar, suspended?
But it's no use.

For me they're just a million
shiny Scrabble tiles flung into space.
For you they are the natives
of a country gathered for dancing,
their rune-spangled map
stored in you like a jewel.

And you're not here to show me
how the stars whisper history,
etch ancient imagination
in their silverpoint,

which leaves me alone.
This is all I am without you:
a squinter into the dark,
necksore and nameless.

the spider isn't attached

a country-sized silence
severs us, severs the one thread
ever stretched between us
thin as spider's web, as entangling
as silver and as full, after dewfall, of tears

do you feel the lurking stickiness
of walking through a spider's web
a trap baited with summer morning
beyond it a cool turning path
with its imagined blackberries
but between you and sweetness
hangs the silver track-stopper
do you jump, hop, brush yourself
hope the spider isn't attached somewhere
riding home on the back of your neck

you're like the bat that got in the house
swooped silently back and forth
across the TV-lighted ceiling
followed me up to the bedroom
and had to have doors and windows left open
to let it back into its native night

it was trapped
it didn't want to be here
it just made a stupid mistake:

my life
a blue-lit nightmare
into which you blundered

"Ah, you who are silent..." Pablo Neruda

You speak, then,
with every mouthless thing.
The sky spreads your pink and red
words out with purpling fingers.

Trees toss your sibilants, your beginnings
and endings, back and forth to one another
across the humming wires of the wind.

Your silence makes a word of every wave.
The foam as each retreats is the breath
that escapes at the end of each word,
the anticipatory breath. The spread lips.

My own face glowering back at me
from the bathroom mirror forms phrases
my head hears in your absent voice.
Those sentences lay themselves, long black
threads of secrets, in every line of my face.

Your silence, as poisonous as mercury,
as weighty and beautiful and quicksilver,
drips with soundless sentences
as it slips away between my empty fingers.

Public Library

I think of you when the walls are covered with books.

Slide along a row of flat spines, slip one out and touch
the much-read pages.

When books' peculiar silence falls over me, that muffled
lovely cloud, everything I need is there.

Everything lives in those many-coloured little houses.
They wait for you. They open with little more than a touch.

They open entirely.

Why does a long aisle of library books make me want you?
People barely murmur here, barely look at one another.

When you find someone alone in an aisle he seems abashed,
almost, and hurries himself away.

All the shelves here beat, pulse, throb with life. The pages hum,
vibrate, sing with it. They almost glow.

The whole place is life bound, corseted, asking you to choose
it, pull it into the air and loosen its stays.

The chaos in my middle is brought to order by an eight-foot
wall of abstracts, annals and indices in their heavy blue coats.

So of course I want you here, but not your words.
Just your body in the quiet tunnel of books.

No skin even, just your warm clothed arms. Your sweatered
torso. Your collarbone curving silently round on itself.

Unable to let each other go, we would be pinned in place,
backs against the books, our arms full of each other,

our mouths closed and silenced by a million tied-up words
crying to be set free from their quiet, quivering cells.

Grey dove

There is the rustling, the stirring of wing-feathers, the quick flowing of the alley dove lost in its dark Jerusalem of rain…
– Russell Thornton, from "Rain City"

It begins on the bus or the train, or in the woods
under morning's lime-green leaves. Anywhere
I've been walking long enough or silent
long enough it can begin, the rustling, the turning
and waking of the sleek grey dove I know
is nesting in the dark inside of me.

She wants to be fed: she wants young things
helpless enough to devour alive. Silent, I give in
almost every time, give her the tender, unborn
things in me. She swallows them whole.

Nightly I follow her flight down streets
of rain-reflected lamplight. We look for
her mate, the mate the grey bird lost long ago,
the grey bird's sweet and soaring other self,
her mirror-bird, broken in pieces when the walls
fell, when the air, smoke-and-bullet-pocked,
hid his rising, then swept him clean away.

No wonder she lives on the embryonic,
all my premature but beating hearts;
where once lived bird and mated bird, now

a half-dove rolls awake, every waking like
the first day she rose without him.

She and I give the most dove-like cry then, quiet
and broken, every day the first arrow in the first breast.

Single Silver Earring

When left alone, I think about myself
too much. How metallic I must smell;
how I would taste of tinfoil.

I miss the tiny *clink clink*
we made when my twin rolled
into me in a warm hand, reassuring
each other we were both there.

But then we would be held up
to the light! We loved the light, and the slow
shift of our own weight slung back and forth.

That sense of rocking replaced even the first
memory: the great heat, the hammering
and the piercing and the knowledge
that we endured it together.

I dream of falling now, of striking the base
of her neck and hitting the ground, staying
still, unworn, lost. Left alone now, I crave
the stillness, the muffled sides, of a blue
velvet box, one to receive and rock to rest
my single hollow body.

May Bluster

Near the end of cottonwood season with a May bluster rushing through, pulling the pods themselves off the trees still full of fuzz, scattering them across the clipped grass like handfuls of chicken feed. Standing among the shedding cottonwoods is all you have energy for now.

It's like being a railway track with a long, long train on it. You're sure the pressure, the almost breaking, will never end, even as you know it will because you've borne this heavy traveller before. The self splits, layers, into the one who feels and the one who knows. Two rails lying parallel.

You can't feel what you know; you can't acknowledge what you feel. Your brittle layers pile one on the other, paleontological.

Oh to be living and whole, like the dark-haired oboist who last week made such a glory of Bach on the red church carpet! You saw her only from behind, her compact brown body moving, kneading the notes up out of the oboe, her legs, back and shoulders, head, neck and arms, all moving in a slight weave, as a flame just breathed on.

The notes and the meaning of the notes rushed all into that sound, the very ink used to scratch out the notes, the air Bach was exhaling the moment he wrote them down – all pulled through her swaying oboe and freed, a whole voice, a whole music.

No layers, fragile as fossils, there. No sediment of sticky indecision, like a dead cottonwood pod clinging to the branch, unable to grow but unable to throw its life to earth. Only the May bluster, the raking wind, can pull it free now. Only the coming storm, with its thunder and thrown hail, can bear it down.

The Wet Edge of the Promised Land

How a groomed beach erases geography,
makes every shore like every other,
as well it should. We don't come here
to stare into the sand.

We come for the ocean,
that one monstrous blue-green animal
who stretches her restless limbs
over all the earth. She is the leviathan
who cannot escape us.

We can't get enough of her.
Tissue-pale in the morning,
a heavy turquoise slab at noon
or red at dusk as she lets go
her issue of blood, we make sure
we're there, near enough to touch her.

For a few minutes we'll even let her
swallow us; we'll even leave a land
crowded with promises. Wordless,
we'll dive into her deeps to listen
to life without a country, to lie slack
in her cool and landless silence.

low tide

low tide, and everything hidden
is now uncovered: the black weed, certainly
but also the upright fields of barnacles fighting
for space with the black mussels, these
gathered like a thousand shiny goat hooves
tied up and down the oily piles

the air is not their native habitat
in the breeze they clamp tight shut
nothing moist and pulsing
must be open to the sunlight

and we admire their defence, breathe
in sweetly their walls' salt smell

when the tide lowers around our own
wet hearts there is no shield to slam
no doors we can clap closed around it
like the lid covers the glittering slick eyeball

no dreaming in briny bone-cells
for our washed up, low tide hearts

while the sun shines, they must lie
still in it, let their tissue-thin skin crack
and curl open, gasping in the open air

tides change
turn and return

barnacles and mussels, even the black
weed crunched in the sand, know
the tide will miss them and come back

our hearts, baking in their cracked-up
hides, lose all knowing, can breathe only
shallowly for reasons they cannot remember
trying not to lose what's left of slippery life

Fruition

One green sphere hanging from a maple branch
sends the point home: one curled crispy leaf
blowing by across the gravel. The starlings' heads
have had their shine baked to a mellow
lilac-grey. Summer runs full bore toward its end.

We chased a colander full of ripe apricots
all the way here but they're turning brown,
letting go a sickly syrup, are aging headlong past eating.
They sit in the fridge. No one wants them now.

We're in wine country, a fertile womb
in a desert. We drive from vineyard to vineyard,
tasting and hoarding every small fruition.
We forget the winepress, the peach pit, the seed
we suck for all its sweetness and throw back into the earth.

Next year we'll come looking for it, the fruit
swelling into damp globes in the leaves' shade.
Don't remind us of the in-between time, the burial,
the silence, the eventual groping up through black mud
toward thaw. We want a dip in the warm lake

this afternoon. We want ripe fruit in the full shade.
We want tanned limbs and colour and sugar and wine.

Osoyoos Lake

The moon hangs askew, rust-coloured,
blood-smeared. It leaks pale red light
onto the lake's black skin.

I remember your face, impassive
in the firelight. I wanted to speak, wanted
to ask and tell, but all that might have tumbled
through me was a cataract, a flood, was
the whole lake we stared at out past the fire.

I was too small.
I watched your face, impassive, orange and red
hands of firelight spread out, stroking it.
Something should have been done right then.
But I say it again: I was too small.

The firelight took your face, the lake,
the darkness on either side of the
blood-coloured light. It closed you in
and carried you away and snapped you shut.

As the Light Fails

Not fails, don't say "fails," but falls, falls;
not sinks, but moves around the earth;
not disappears, but takes itself otherwhere,
a white hat tugged rakishly across the world's head.

As it does all those things, the massive light,
the wine bottle empties itself into the darkness.

Even after you back away into the night
the wine keeps pouring itself, an indigo gold now,
into the glass, into my throat, into whatever part of me
I'm willing to deliver up to the night right then.

Which is pretty much every part, the dipper
tipped low to receive me in the northern sky,
the young eagle asleep in his bowl of black branches.

Stars make a web over me, a web of light, its silks
stretched so thin you'd never see it, but it catches
us. Wherever we are, it has us in its web, day and night.

Light is a sweet, sweet spider. She fills us full
of herself, one silver thread at a time. She never sleeps.
Night plays the line out, falling slowly over our shoulders
as the cool air rises; night carries a lace of light too fine
to see, but it keeps us warm. It keeps us going.

It keeps us in the air somehow, on the same migratory
flight; somehow aloft on the same pair of ink-dark wings.

Eating the Fruit

The removal of your love (a plant uprooted)
has not changed the bloom on the grapes' skins;
the assertion of the mango cubes, an aroused orange;
the white plate flawless, its oval holding
nothing but two perfect grains of blond sugar.

Wherever your love has gone, the fruit here
continues sweet, and the coffee too,
as sweet and as hot as we need it,
for the sun has covered itself with clouds.
It ripened the pineapples, the strawberries
in the field, the grapes, the honeydew, then
saw the harvesters at hand and retreated.

So the light on the last piece of mango
is a greyed, a diluted light. I take the last bite,
the white bowl holding just a rime of syrup.
Then the plate, the bowl, the proportional fork
laid across it. The meal a perfection of emptiness.

wine glass

has risen above
the rest of the vessels
on its single crystal leg

its hips blooming
all around itself
open, clear, hollow

a mouth that never
speaks but never closes
perpetually agape

to take in what falls
in from over its head
the red and the white

sometimes it's filled
with blood that's cooled
almost to freezing

then it breathes
and keeps its silence
and covers itself with tears

The Open Book

When you were young and your heart was an open book...
— Paul McCartney

No, no, that's backward. When I was young
my heart's pages were all stuck together
with peanut butter and strawberry lip gloss
and if you'd been able to pry them apart
whatever sad scrawls you found there
would sound like mid-seventies' AM radio lyrics:

Love, one page may have said. *Love me. Kiss me*,
the next may have said. *I'd kiss you perfectly
if you gave me the chance. Arms*, I may have
written. *I have a pair waiting, warm and empty.*

I could go on, list all the greasy pages you may have
found there, every sticky word: *look, touch, dance,
darkness.* I could string together the right words
but I was a parrot, performing noises I couldn't
understand. Odds are I wrote: *eyes, hands, lips.*
It's possible I wrote them all in my fresh blood.

Aren't we glad that sad old book is long gone
so we never have to know exactly what was there?
We can stop wondering about words like *run*
and *stop* and *hold me*. We know what's become
of them now, and of the heart, whose pages
have taken years to dry and part and open
to the prevailing wind. Her leaves turn

quickly, with barely a breeze, and all the words
that stuck there when she was young
have met the air and blown away, barely
visible, a few smashed flakes of dark ink.

Letters

I write you long letters. They take months,
years, to make it to you. They travel by lost book
and on foot across water. They roll across
town to you on the sides of tossed coffee cups.

I write you long letters with breath, carbon dioxide
inked white against the night sky, you wouldn't believe it;
letters that never seem to end, like *Ulysses*, food and death
and the sea and love and not a little blasphemy (yes yes yes).

Some of my letters are like the glasses of water
served in restaurants: written in icy condensation
and moist fingerprints and holding more than you could
ever hope to take in without a trip to the bathroom.

I do send them, these letters, all unfinished
through the ether, less substantial even than email,
words tipped up and sling-shot into heaven,
Their PPPPSes trailing behind them for a week.

Time-lapse Video

You've given yourself, on every plane,
to time and to its rushing.

Your body complying somehow with my dreams,
losing its cohesion, becoming a speeding mist
pushed along just above the earth, a hurrying cloud.

You want to twist away from me, become a blur,
the face of anyone, neck curled into any bent elbow.

You want to wipe yourself out of me and become a blur,
time held back by a box until space melts into mere
      movement.

You want to melt, become the pattern in the wallpaper,
the shadow of a door ajar, a two-dimensional spill
of watery ink on a moment's onionskin page.

At what moment does the body become a smudge,
a pool of thumb-wiped colour bleeding into another pool?

The Solitude

And here is the solitude from which you are absent
And it is raining…

— Pablo Neruda

So the solitude is a double emptiness,
a ring of air inside a ring of air
held fast in a net of wet branches
glued to the wet pavement.
The space where you are not
and the space where I am
are equally empty spaces.

So much time has passed that your absence
is like a person present with me. I talk to it.
I tell it things; it is the perfect secret keeper.

Who but the absent, the lost, the half-forgotten
could understand this late spring rain, this
chill pulling May into soggy June, these
handfuls of dripping weeds, this silver-grey
evening, this falling, thinning trail of leaden light?

Reading

I am reading R.S. Thomas.
How I pray his wonderful words
will pin me to you somehow like a note,
a reminder, like an odd bit of bus ticket
you find in the inside pocket of a jacket:
you find suddenly that day, that ride,
that time, spilt on you all at once, bracing
and waking and blessing you.
Whatever I am I hope it's blessing you.

Soon I'll walk out into the city streets again.
Eat again. Open my mouth and speak to people
again (sad, sad). Until then all I am is the sum
of my words. All I am is what I'm writing here.
Until I get up to go I can give you all I am,
here at this little black table. Meagre, yes,
but there they are: words, thoughts, prayers,
all in a little handful I save for you.

I am a tiny girl (tiny girl again at heart's door)
offering a dandelion to a demi-god. Whatever
of human love is allowed to be worship
("with my body I thee worship") I offer you
while I sit alone at this little black table.

Whatever in me is discrete, closed off, grown askew
in aloneness, I offer to you, small as it is sure to be.
A bonsai love: a whole tree forced low, bent but blooming.

Some Couplets

Our eyes don't change.
Our eyes are the same when we die.

Each hour shaves a bit off your sternum,
trying to bare your heart.

For years I tried to peel off my name,
but there was always another one underneath.

They bounce down the lane like old leaves,
fragile and finely curled.

You have not imagined, yet,
a world in which someone loves you.

Pretend you've had more sleep
than you have. Someday your body may believe you.

Reflection on Lines by Hakim Sanai

"I have broken my faith a thousand times…"

As though my faith were a sea of glass
And all the years of my life were spent
in an ice-breaker, sailing it into shards.

As though my faith were a whale
I could not stop harpooning.

As though my faith were a tree, and all
my mad desires a hundred swinging hatchets,
my impatience the chipper spitting out matchwood.

"…to meet always with Your forgiveness."

Your furnace that remoulds bright glass
out of the sand of my sailing.

Your deep-sea diving that reanimates
flesh and stops up salted wounds.

Your wide greenhouse
where you find seeds in the splinters,
and set them in moist soil, and wait.

The Jazz Path

Life used to have a trajectory, like being
shot triumphantly from someone's bow.
Not this shuffle, this scant-aired wandering;
not this timid step-toe-heel of dawdling hours.

Even jazz musicians, who sound for all the world
like wanderers, have a *path*, one they skirt
and dodge and parallel, but it's a path.

The jazz path is this season's way, sunlight
filtered and patchy, branches snapping
back at you. I keep watching the earth,
brow furled like Miles Davis, to keep
from tripping over roots rising and
criss-crossing in the unexpected silences.

Miles Davis had a path: a jump on and off the road,
a skip, samba, point-shoe along, dragging himself
from bass to treble, the trumpet muted with a hat
of dust and tears, but feet moving, eyes not even
needing to see, knowing exactly where to step next.

Maybe that's why I crave constant jazz now.
It's a path winding through warm gnarly trees
and twisting back across a meadow of poppies.
Jazz isn't a stroll, a driveway, a clear-cut
that mows down whatever's in the road. It goes
around; it takes the scenic route; it jogs up and down
the hill; runs on the spot to gaze at clouds.

I've been looking back, fighting off a longing
for hymnody, chant, some Hallelujah metre.
But those are too heavy at the moment, too much
of a burden splintering the shoulders.

So the jazz path will do tonight, slipped down my throat
with enough wine to play me toward it: the meander,
la passeggiata, crazy constitutional under the stars,
start and stop and kiss-me-before-we-take-off, baby.

It gets them there in the end. They always fall, laughing,
back into melody, back on to the path, soon enough
for the well-remembered, footsore, sweet refrain.

Scab picker

Blood has dried
in a pleasing ridge, thick
as a fingernail, across a field
of sad plum bruises.

The edges of it hang on like old Band-Aids,
stretching the skin silver before it tears.

The long scab, held by one end
and peeled slowly up, cracks and oozes,
the purple skin beneath
edging itself in lilac as the ridge retreats.

Blood rushes to the place, finds its way
out only through the odd unhealed cells:
there, a dozen pinpoints of liquid red, like mites.

Rip the thing up quickly, as you would uproot
a loose weed. Unstick the Tupperware-tight
seal; let blood surface and make its escape.

Let newborn skin shine
and cry redness in the naked air.

Winter Rewrite

With darkness he returns, and his terrible strength
is wild in that song, like a black wine.

— Osip Mandelstam

I invite your shadow along, invite it even
to replace my own shadow, your name
to be written darkly over my name, pressed hard,
gone over many times to obscure my name,
spindly and faint underneath it.

I would be happy there, an open book.
Your name advances toward my new lines
swiftly, your words catching up with mine
and blotting them out. I have invited this.
It is what I asked for and what has pursued me.

The black wine is ink, then. Permanent ink.
I understand this now. Even understanding this
I drink it down. It's not as bitter as I feared.

To the world it looks as if it filled the veins
like embalming fluid. But be assured; the wine
is doing its work: leaves and leaves of paper
are uncurling all over the inside of the body,
each one being written and rewritten on, black
line after black line in a firm, architectural hand.

It is what I asked for, what I long imagined
being built in me. On all the walls inside me
I feel nib against paper, a black bird's persistent pale claw.

A Quilt

Who will tie off the last few threads, finish
this crazy quilt of years, its panels spun
and woven; its cotton, wool, damask and silk?

Voices and time and searching eyes
have stitched these ragbag remnants,
uneven rectangles, into a landscape:
black for gravitas; multicoloured knits,
afghan-like, for warmth, and silken cords,
red and dark brown, green, blue and gold,
all around its borders:
colours of grains, fruits, October trees.

It is a country of fertile little fields, each
an hour, and dozens of moments, too,
French knots tied in silver punctuating
the many shapes of days and darknesses.

It's a keepsake spread across the back
of the couch, a place to rest my cheek
while I read a book in the dip of quiet
between afternoon and evening.

It's a cover for a whole shivering self,
a shield, a suit of soft armour against January,
February, their army of icy knives.

It's to raise and hang on a wall and admire,
both a small country and that country's

flag, a coat of arms, of many weeping colours,
a standard under which I have agreed to march;
a heavy pennant; a silent, blazing banner.

Three Things on the Winter Ground

Moss: emeralds have sprung out of the earth,
embraceable, rain and dew their blood,
the gathered sweetness of melancholic shade.

Leaves: the grass is full of skeletal hands
the trees have dropped, weary with summer reaching.
Brown fingers, dry with grasping, let all fall.

Stone: in wall or cairn, in path or mountain,
a stone is a promise, is history in the hand.
Crack open the earth and find again the earth.

Heart

The heart rests on its bed, a quiet place.
It sits, silent and post-surgical.
Recovering from itself, it hides its face.

Don't drag it out too soon to join the chase.
Guard it while its stitches are still damp.
The heart rests on its bed, a quiet place.

Don't be in such a hurry to unlace
the burka out of which its black eyes shine.
Recovering from itself, it hides its face.

Be careful of its wounds; give them their space.
They speak out of the shadow of its name.
The heart rests on its bed, a quiet place.

The heart will knit, will heal at its own pace.
Spring can't come until the winter's spent.
Recovering from itself, it hides its face.

All the heart needs is your mute embrace,
your patient presence, convalescent love.
The heart rests on its bed, a quiet place.
Recovering from itself, it hides its face.

A Protestant Talks to Mary

Lady, the night has got us by the heart...
— Thomas Merton

Both of us, then, have a heart. Yours
(perfected and sacred now, they say)
was pocked once like mine, abashed, frightened,
lost and clueless as a new queen on a dungheap.

The night can still get me, and you too, it seems.
Though when it presses your heart, extra virgin
oil pours out and anoints whatever is near it.
It turns dry bread into dinner. Whatever was stuck,
whatever was rusted, it soothes and loosens.

When the night takes hold of me and squeezes,
there's just hot air: a sigh, walls crumbling, dust.

Technically I'm not on your team, lady,
but I'll go to bat for you: your mouth
is a haloed glory, every branch of you
pregnantly round and ruddy with blossom.
Your perfected heart drops flowers after rain.

Our Lord is drawing us, day by day, out from
under night's black mud. We'll both finish
young, tender, full forever of cool light and fresh
juices, awestruck lilies perpetually in bloom.

Basilique Notre Dame, Ottawa

My life: bits of smashed
glass
in a bloody mire.

I lift them up here. My
arms
seem very long today.

Up go all the filthy fragments
of me
into the royal buttressed blue.

Look! Fistfuls of dirty shards
arise
and come down again as stars,

as a constellation: my life
arrayed
behind and before,

all her molecules
scoured
and reassembled,

a jewelled system in the
dark air,
imperceptibly orbiting.

Acknowledgments

Poems from this collection first appeared in:

On Spec

Prism International

Harvard Review

The Puritan

Event

The Fourth River

Arc

Crux

Rhythm

paperplates

The Absinthe Literary Review

The Nashwaak Review